Are Crop Circles Real?

BY ALLISON LASSIEUR

AMICUS HIGH INTEREST ❖ AMICUS INK

Amicus High Interest and Amicus Ink are imprints of Amicus
P.O. Box 1329, Mankato, MN 56002
www.amicuspublishing.us

Library of Congress Cataloging-in-Publication Data
Lassieur, Allison.
 Are crop circles real? / by Allison Lassieur.
    pages cm. — (Unexplained: what's the evidence?)
Includes index.
 Summary: "Presents stories of crop circles, designs that appear
in crop fields, often overnight. Examines the evidence of various
explanations"— Provided by publisher.
 ISBN 978-1-60753-804-2 (library binding) —
 ISBN 978-1-60753-893-6 (e-book)
 ISBN 978-1-68152-045-2 (paperback)
 1. Crop circles. I. Title.
 AG243.L34 2016
 001.94—dc23

                                    2014038739

Series Editor   Rebecca Glaser
Series Designer   Kathleen Petelinsek
Book Designer   Heather Dreisbach
Photo Researcher   Derek Brown

Photo Credits: Steve Alexander Photography, Cover; Trinity
Mirror/Mirrorpix/Alamy, 5; teslamax/iStock, 6; Jon Arnold
Images Ltd/Alamy, 9; Wikimedia Commons Public Domain, 10;
Hoberman Collection/Corbis, 13; Mike Agliolo/Corbis, 14;
SUSAN TUSA/DETROIT FREE PRESS/ASSOCIATED PRESS,
17; Avella/Shutterstock, 18; Heritage Image Partnership Ltd/
Alamy, 21; Trinity Mirror/Mirrorpix/Alamy, 22; Trinity Mirror/
Mirrorpix/Alamy, 25; Colin Underhill/Alamy, 26; Splash
News/Corbis, 29

Printed in Malaysia

HC 10 9 8 7 6 5 4 3 2 1
PB 10 9 8 7 6 5 4 3 2 1

Table of Contents

What Is a Crop Circle?

It was July of 1990. A farmer named Tim Carson went into his field. He was shocked! A huge area of corn plants was flattened. Other plants were left standing. This made a **design**. These designs are called crop circles. The crop circle in Carson's field became famous around the world.

Tim Carson was amazed to find this design in his field.

In 2009, this crop circle showed up in front of a castle in Italy.

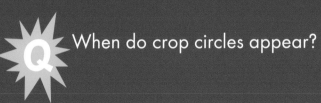

Q When do crop circles appear?

Crop circles often appear in one night. No clues tell how they were made. Some crop circles are simple. They are just plain circles. Other crop circles are more **complex**. One crop circle can have hundreds of shapes. The edges of a crop circle are very clean. They look like a machine made them.

They show up when crops are growing, usually in summer.

Crop circles are found all over the world. American farmers have seen crop circles in their fields. But most crop circles appear in south England. That part of England is very old. Many crop circles appear near **ancient** stones and mounds there. No one is sure why.

Crop circles are seen near ancient stones in southern England.

8

In the oldest crop circle story,
the devil cut down the crops.

Licenſed, *Auguſt* 22th. 1678.

 What is another name for a crop circle?

First Reports

Crop circles are not new. One story is more than 300 years old. In the story, a crop circle was made by the devil! After that, farmers saw other crop circles. These circles appeared year after year. Farmers did not think the devil made those circles. But they were common. No one thought much about them.

 People used to call them "devil's twists" and "corn circles."

In 1966, a farmer in Australia said he saw flying saucers in a swamp. They made circles in the grasses. This report did not get much attention.

In August 1980, a farmer in England went to his fields. He found three huge crop circles. A local newspaper told the story. The news spread quickly.

In Australia, large circles of flattened grasses were seen in a swamp like this one.

Some people thought that UFOs made crop circles.

Q What is a person who studies crop circles called?

Suddenly lots of people wanted to know about crop circles. Some people thought that **aliens** made the crop circles. **UFO** scientists rushed to the field. They studied the flattened plants. Each year after that, people found more crop circles in southern England. Many people went there to see the crop circles.

 A **cereologist**. The word comes from the Roman goddess Ceres. She was the goddess of **agriculture**.

More crop circles showed up every year. They got bigger and more complex. A **meteorologist** named Dr. George Terrence Meaden studied the crop circles. He said they were made by swirling winds. He called this wind a **plasma vortex**. Some people agreed. Others did not. The circles were a huge mystery.

A farmer in Michigan examines a crop circle in his wheat field.

Many crop circles have appeared near Stonehenge.

 What is Stonehenge?

Crop Circle at Stonehenge

The biggest crop circle story happened in July 1996 in England. A doctor wanted to see Stonehenge. He hired a pilot. They flew over Stonehenge once. It was late afternoon. The fields nearby were normal. The pilot flew over again. Now there was a crop circle in the field!

 A stone circle made of huge standing stones. People built it more than 5,000 years ago.

People stopped their cars to see the crop circle. Some people saw a strange mist in the field. The mist got bigger. Then the crop circle got bigger! The circles were made in just a few seconds. It was the first report of anyone seeing a crop circle being made. The pattern was a spiral. It had 149 circles! It was called the Julia set.

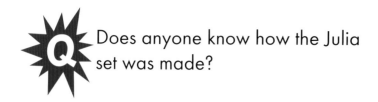 Does anyone know how the Julia set was made?

The Julia set design is based on a complex math equation.

Not for sure. Some people said that humans made it the night before. The pilot didn't notice it the first time he flew over.

Doug Bower shows off his plans for crop circle designs.

 Q How many crop circles did Doug and Dave make?

Exposing the Fakes

Crop circles are real. There is no doubt about that. But how were crop circles made? Who made them? Those were the big mysteries. In 1991, two men named Doug Bower and Dave Chorley came forward. They said crop circles were a **hoax**. They had made crop circles. They wanted people to believe that aliens had come to Earth.

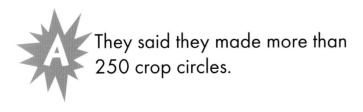
They said they made more than 250 crop circles.

Doug and Dave showed how they made the crop circles. They tied a rope to a plank of wood. They stepped on the plank. The plank flattened the plants. Everyone said the mystery was solved. Later other crop circle makers came forward. Today we know that people make most crop circles.

 What is the plank and rope tool called?

Doug Bower stomped on a plank of wood to make crop circles.

 Circle artists call the wood plank a "stalk stomper."

Plant stems are bent, not cut, to make crop circles.

What's the Evidence?

Thousands of crop circles have been found around the world. Experts say they can tell which ones are man-made. The plants are broken. They may find footprints there. But some crop circles can't be explained. The plant stems are bent, but not crushed. The plants seem to be burnt. How these crop circles are made is still a mystery.

Some people still think that UFOs make crop circles. Or maybe they are a message from aliens. People say they have seen balls of light before crop circles appear. Could powerful energy in the earth make crop circles? No one can prove these ideas. But everyone can agree on one thing. Crop circles are beautiful and mysterious.

This man-made crop circle appeared in Wiltshire, England, in 2012. It shows a polar clock.

Glossary

agriculture The science of growing crops.

alien A creature from another planet.

ancient Very old; having lived or existed for a long time.

cereologist A person who studies crop circles.

complex Having many parts.

design A plan or drawing.

hoax A trick to make someone believe something that is not true.

meteorologist A scientist who studies the weather.

plasma vortex Swirling wind filled with electricity.

polar clock A design that uses arcs and circles to measure different units of time.

UFO An unidentified flying object, sometimes thought to be a spaceship from another planet.

Read More

Bingham, Jane. *Crop Circles*. Chicago: Capstone Raintree, 2013.

Burns, Jan. *Crop Circles*. Detroit: KidHaven Press, 2008.

Helstrom, Kraig. *Crop Circles*. Minneapolis: Bellwether Media, 2011.

Martin, Michael. *Crop Circles*. Mankato, Minn.: Capstone Press, 2006.

Websites

DOGONews: "Alien" Crop Circles Are Back!
*http://www.dogonews.com/2010/5/10/
alien-crop-circles-are-back*

National Geographic: Crop Circles:
Crop Circle Creation
*http://channel.nationalgeographic.com/channel/videos/
crop-circle-creation/*

Index

About the Author

Allison Lassieur loves reading and writing about strange, mysterious, and unusual places in the world. She has written more than 150 books for kids, and she also likes to write about history, food, and science. Allison lives in a house in the woods with her husband, daughter, three dogs, two cats, and a blue fish named Marmalade.